Times Tables Practice

Exercises devised by David Kirkby
a senior lecturer in Mathematics Education at
Sheffield Hallam University
Illustrated by John Haslam

Learning Rewards is a home-learning programme designed to help your child succeed at school with the National Curriculum. It has been extensively researched with parents and teachers.

This book, *Times Tables Practice*, and its companion title, *Times Tables Skills*, cover important aspects of the National Curriculum at Key Stage I.

Children should start with the *Skills* books (with younger children this is important) and progress to the *Practice* books.

The *Skills* book teaches basic skills and new concepts through structured and enjoyable activities. The *Practice* book reinforces and builds on these skills by the essential repetition of exercises.

You will need to work through each page with your child and talk about what is required. The star symbol at the top of the page details the particular skills covered by the exercise as they relate to the National Curriculum. The content is progressive, so explain the importance of starting from the front of the book.

The fold-out progress chart is a useful record of your child's performance. Always reward your child's work with encouragement and a gold star sticker.

When you come to the end of the book you will find a fun, wipe-clean learning game.

series editor: Nina Filipek
series designer: Paul Dronsfield
Copyright © 1996 World International Limited.
All rights reserved.
Published in Great Britain by
World International Limited, Deanway Technology Centre,
Wilmslow Road, Handforth, Cheshire SK9 3FB.
Printed in Italy.
ISBN 0 7498 2715 7

Times Tables

Twos

 To multiply by 2.

Write in the missing numbers.

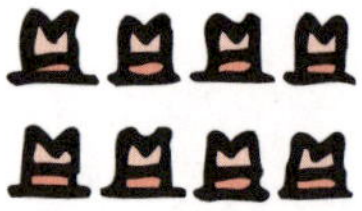

2 rows of [4]   [4] x 2 = [8]

2 rows of [5]   [5] x 2 = [10]

2 rows of [ ]   [ ] x 2 = [ ]

2 rows of [ ]   [ ] x 2 = [ ]

2 rows of [ ]   [ ] x 2 = [ ]

2 rows of [ ]   [ ] x 2 = [ ]

1 x 2 = 2	2 x 2 =	3 x 2 =	4 x 2 =	5 x 2 =
6 x 2 =	7 x 2 =	8 x 2 =	9 x 2 =	10 x 2 =

Times Tables

To multiply by 2.

Twos

Write in the missing numbers.

 1 cat 2 ears   1 x 2 = 2

 4 cats ☐ ears ☐ x 2 = ☐

 3 cats ☐ ears ☐ x 2 = ☐

 7 cats ☐ ears ☐ x 2 = ☐

 2 cats ☐ ears ☐ x 2 = ☐

Complete the table.

In	6	2	9	10	5	8	4	1
Out	12							

Times Tables

Twos

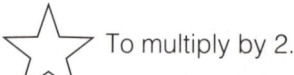 To multiply by 2.

Complete the number sentences.

3 x 2 = 6

7 x 2 =

8 x 2 =

4 x 2 =

5 x 2 =

10 x 2 =

6 x 2 =

9 x 2 =

Write numbers in the grid on the right by multiplying by 2.

2	8	6	4
4	3	1	9
7	10	5	6
5	0	7	8

x 2 →

4	16		

4

Times Tables

☆ To multiply by 3.

Threes

Write in the missing numbers.

 3 rows of [4] [4] x 3 = [12]

 3 rows of [ ] [ ] x 3 = [ ]

 3 rows of [ ] [ ] x 3 = [ ]

 3 rows of [ ] [ ] x 3 = [ ]

 3 rows of [ ] [ ] x 3 = [ ]

 3 rows of [ ] [ ] x 3 = [ ]

1 x 3 = 3	2 x 3 =	3 x 3 =	4 x 3 =	5 x 3 =
6 x 3 =	7 x 3 =	8 x 3 =	9 x 3 =	10 x 3 =

Times Tables

Threes

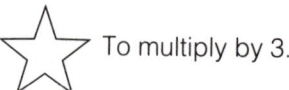 To multiply by 3.

Write in the missing numbers.

 1 triangle [3] corners [1] x 3 = [3]

 5 triangles [ ] corners [ ] x 3 = [ ]

 6 triangles [ ] corners [ ] x 3 = [ ]

 4 triangles [ ] corners [ ] x 3 = [ ]

 2 triangles [ ] corners [ ] x 3 = [ ]

Complete the table.

In	6	10	3	7	2	8	5	9
Out	18							

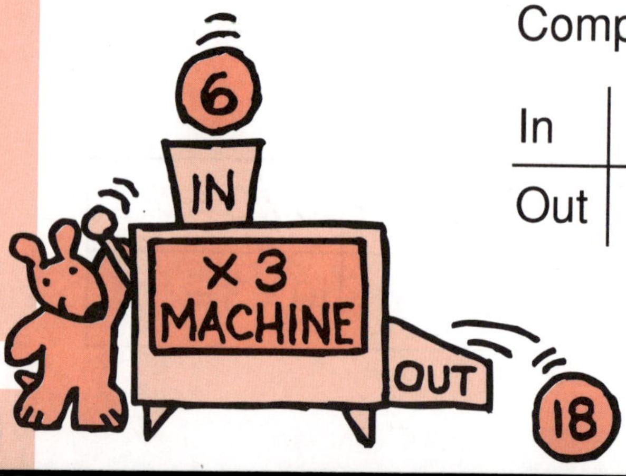

Times Tables

Threes

☆ To multiply by 3.

Complete the multiplications.

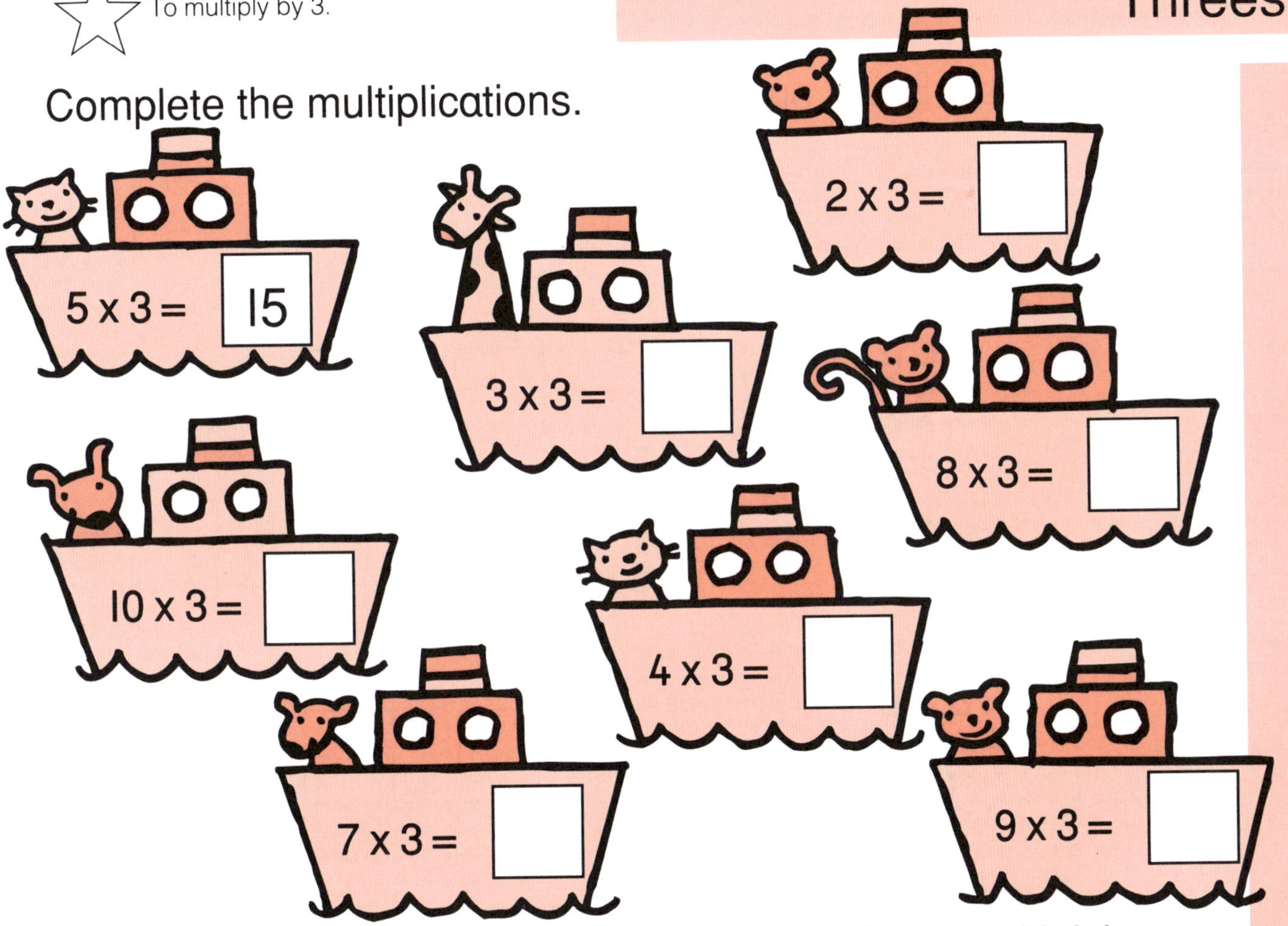
5 x 3 = 15
3 x 3 =
2 x 3 =
8 x 3 =
10 x 3 =
4 x 3 =
7 x 3 =
9 x 3 =

Write numbers in the honeycomb on the right by multiplying by 3.

10
1
2
5
8
6
9
7
4
3
4
0
8
6
7
3
x 3
30
3

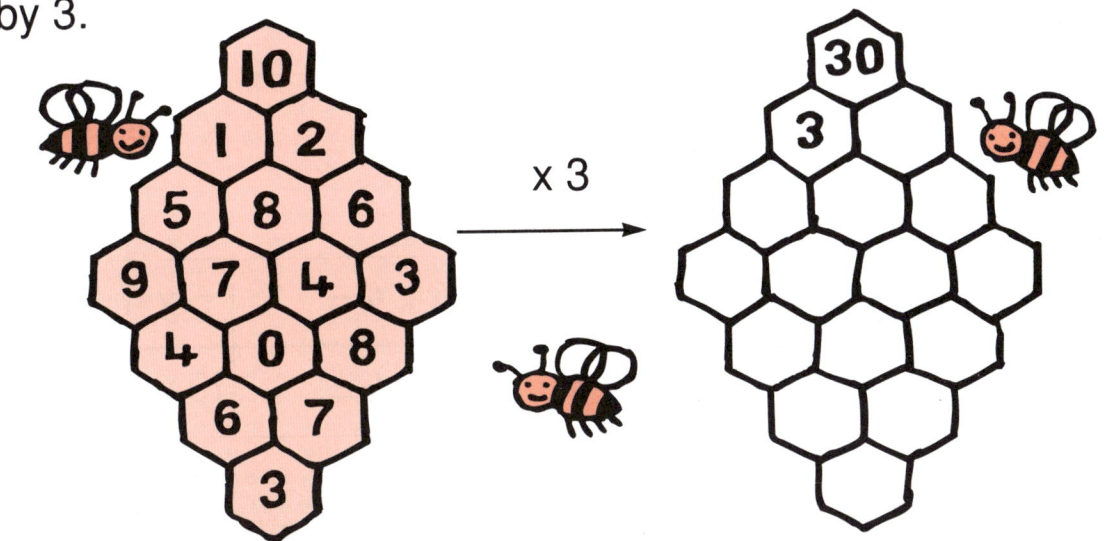

Times Tables

Fours

To multiply by 4.

Write in the missing numbers.

 4 rows of 5   5 x 4 = 20

 4 rows of [ ]   [ ] x 4 = [ ]

 4 rows of [ ]   [ ] x 4 = [ ]

4 rows of [ ]   [ ] x 4 = [ ]

4 rows of [ ]   [ ] x 4 = [ ]

 4 rows of [ ]   [ ] x 4 = [ ]

1 x 4 = 4	2 x 4 =	3 x 4 =	4 x 4 =	5 x 4 =
6 x 4 =	7 x 4 =	8 x 4 =	9 x 4 =	10 x 4 =

Times Tables

Fours

 To multiply by 4.

Write in the missing numbers.

  1 square | 4 | corners | 1 | × 4 = | 4 |

 3 squares | | corners | | × 4 = | |

 7 squares | | corners | | × 4 = | |

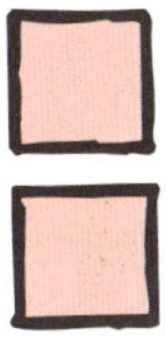

 2 squares | | corners | | × 4 = | |

 5 squares | | corners | | × 4 = | |

Complete the table.

In	2	9	7	5	10	4	6	8
Out	8							

Times Tables

Fours

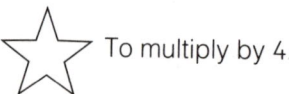 To multiply by 4.

Complete the number sentences.

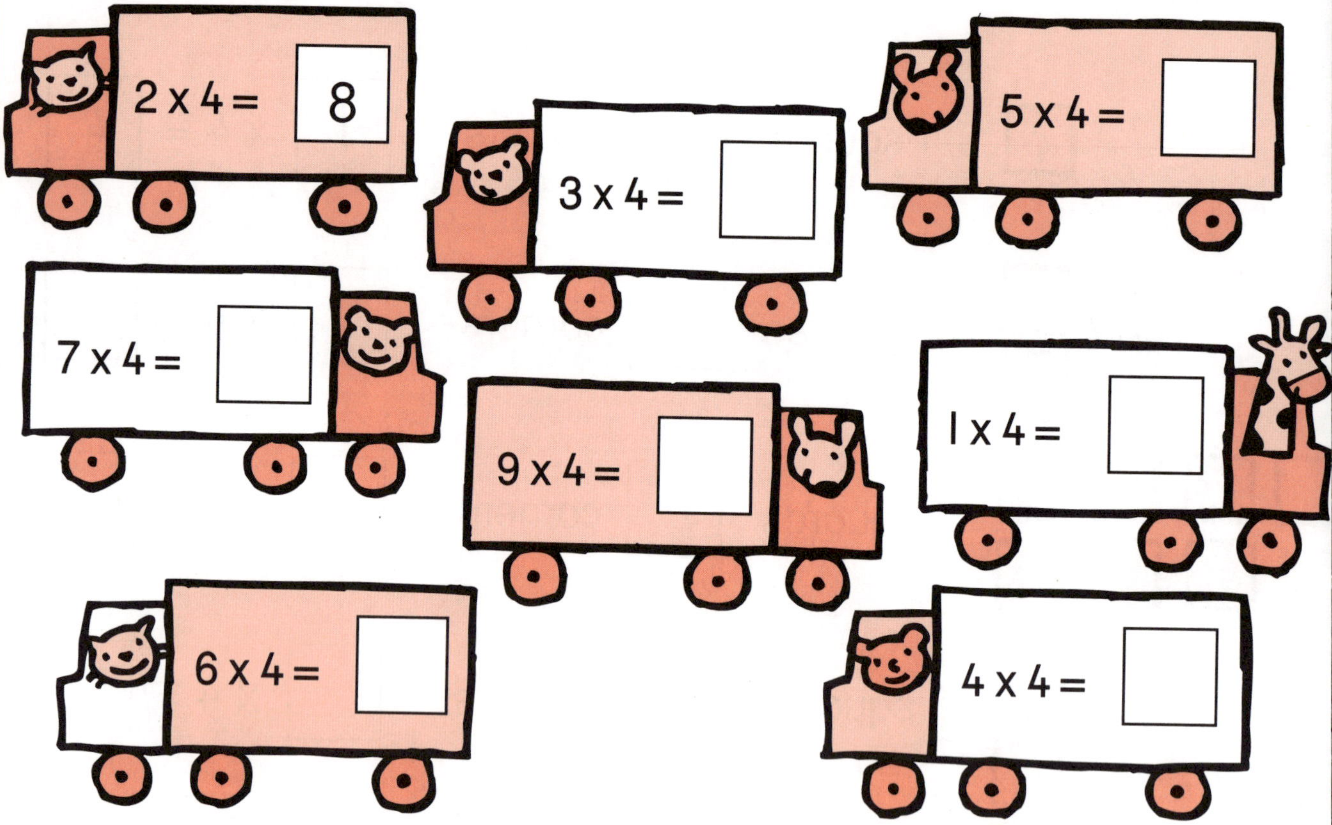

2 x 4 = 8

3 x 4 =

5 x 4 =

7 x 4 =

9 x 4 =

1 x 4 =

6 x 4 =

4 x 4 =

Write numbers in the grid on the right by multiplying by 4.

6	3	10	2
5	1	4	8
4	9	0	3
2	5	6	7

x 4 →

24	12		

Times Tables

☆ To double a number.

Doubling

All darts in the ring count double.
Write down the scores for these darts.

scores 6 x 2 = 12

scores ☐ x 2 = ☐

scores ☐ x 2 = ☐

scores ☐ x 2 = ☐

scores ☐ x 2 = ☐

scores ☐ x 2 = ☐

Complete the table.

In	3	5	7	2	8	4	9	6
Out	6							

Times Tables

Trebling

 To treble a number.

All darts in the ring count treble.
Write down the scores for these darts.

 scores [4] x 3 = [12]

 scores [ ] x 3 = [ ]

 scores [ ] x 3 = [ ]

 scores [ ] x 3 = [ ]

 scores [ ] x 3 = [ ]

 scores [ ] x 3 = [ ]

Complete the table.

In	5	8	6	10	4	9	7	3
Out	15							

Times Tables

Fives

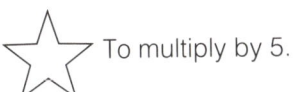 To multiply by 5.

Write in the missing numbers.

5 rows of [5] [5] x 5 = [25]

5 rows of [ ] [ ] x 5 = [ ]

5 rows of [ ] [ ] x 5 = [ ]

5 rows of [ ] [ ] x 5 = [ ]

5 rows of [ ] [ ] x 5 = [ ]

5 rows of [ ] [ ] x 5 = [ ]

1 x 5 = 5	2 x 5 =	3 x 5 =	4 x 5 =	5 x 5 =
6 x 5 =	7 x 5 =	8 x 5 =	9 x 5 =	10 x 5 =

Times Tables

Fives

 To multiply by 5.

Write in the missing numbers.

 1 pentagon [5] corners [1] x 5 = [5]

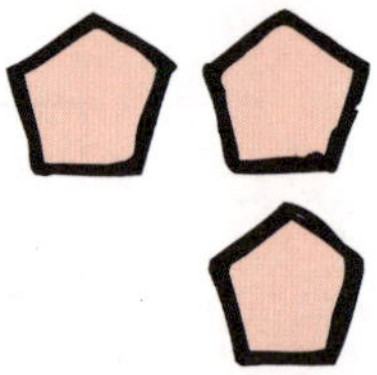

 3 pentagons [ ] corners [ ] x 5 = [ ]

 6 pentagons [ ] corners [ ] x 5 = [ ]

 5 pentagons [ ] corners [ ] x 5 = [ ]

 2 pentagons [ ] corners [ ] x 5 = [ ]

Complete the table.

In	3	7	4	9	2	8	5	10
Out	15							

14

Times Tables

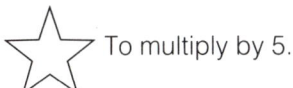 To multiply by 5.

Fives

Complete the multiplications.

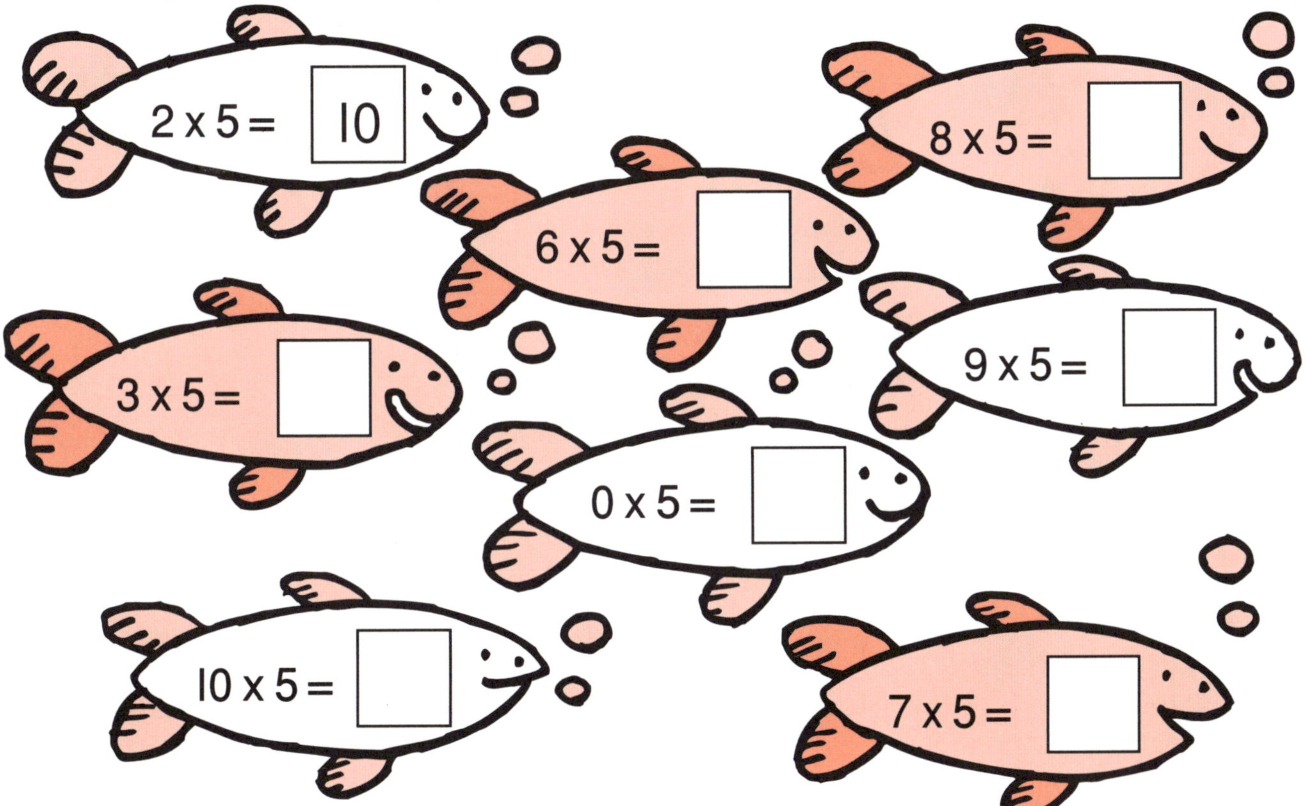

2 x 5 = 10

8 x 5 = ☐

6 x 5 = ☐

3 x 5 = ☐

9 x 5 = ☐

0 x 5 = ☐

10 x 5 = ☐

7 x 5 = ☐

Write numbers in the honeycomb on the right by multiplying by 5.

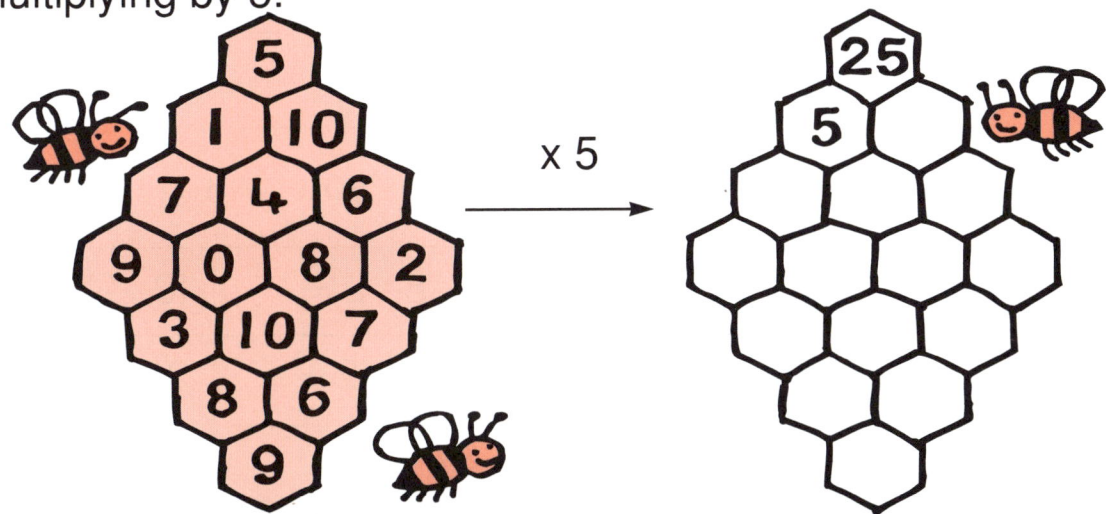

Times Tables

Sharing between two

☆ To divide by 2.

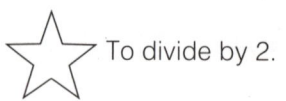

Share these shapes between two by drawing them.

| 8 | shared by 2 is | 4 | each | 8 | ÷ 2 = | 4 |

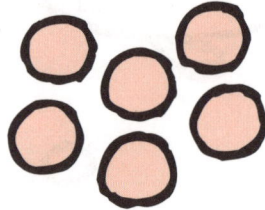

| ☐ | shared by 2 is | ☐ | each | ☐ | ÷ 2 = | ☐ |

| ☐ | shared by 2 is | ☐ | each | ☐ | ÷ 2 = | ☐ |

Complete the table. Say each sum when you write it.

2 ÷ 2 = 1	4 ÷ 2 =	6 ÷ 2 =	8 ÷ 2 =	10 ÷ 2 =
12 ÷ 2 =	14 ÷ 2 =	16 ÷ 2 =	18 ÷ 2 =	20 ÷ 2 =

Times Tables

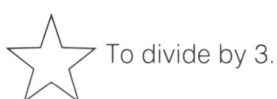 To divide by 3.

Sharing between three

Share these shapes between three by drawing them.

| 6 | shared by 3 is | 2 | each | | 6 | ÷ 3 = | 2 |

| | shared by 3 is | | each | | | ÷ 3 = | |

| | shared by 3 is | | each | | | ÷ 3 = | |

Complete the table. Say each sum when you write it.

3 ÷ 3 = 1	6 ÷ 3 =	9 ÷ 3 =	12 ÷ 3 =	15 ÷ 3 =
18 ÷ 3 =	21 ÷ 3 =	24 ÷ 3 =	27 ÷ 3 =	30 ÷ 3 =

Times Tables

Coins

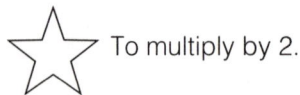 To multiply by 2.

These are piles of 2p coins. Write down how much money there is in each pile.

 ☐ 5 ☐ x 2p = ☐ 10p ☐    ☐ x 2p = ☐

 ☐ x 2p = ☐   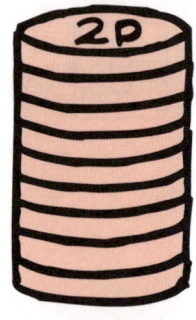 ☐ x 2p = ☐

 ☐ x 2p = ☐    ☐ x 2p = ☐

 ☐ x 2p = ☐    ☐ x 2p = ☐

Complete the table.

1 x 2p = 2p	2 x 2p =	3 x 2p =	4 x 2p =	5 x 2p =
6 x 2p =	7 x 2p =	8 x 2p =	9 x 2p =	10 x 2p =

Times Tables

☆ To multiply by 5.

Coins

These are piles of 5p coins. Write down how much money there is in each pile.

 3 x 5p = 15p    ☐ x 5p = ☐

 ☐ x 5p = ☐    ☐ x 5p = ☐

 ☐ x 5p = ☐    ☐ x 5p = ☐

 ☐ x 5p = ☐   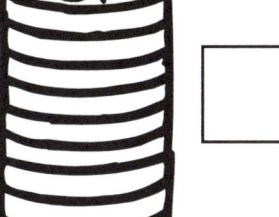 ☐ x 5p = ☐

Complete the table.

1 x 5p = 5p	2 x 5p =	3 x 5p =	4 x 5p =	5 x 5p =
6 x 5p =	7 x 5p =	8 x 5p =	9 x 5p =	10 x 5p =

Times Tables

Tens

 To multiply by 10.

Write in the missing numbers.

  1 tower   10   cubes   1   x 10 =   10

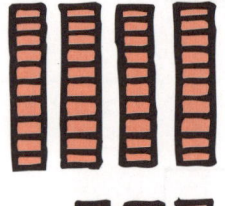 4 towers   [ ] cubes   [ ] x 10 = [ ]

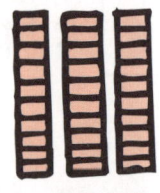 3 towers   [ ] cubes   [ ] x 10 = [ ]

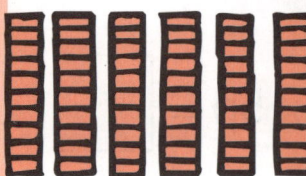 7 towers   [ ] cubes   [ ] x 10 = [ ]

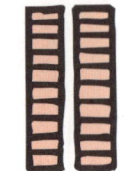 2 towers   [ ] cubes   [ ] x 10 = [ ]

Complete the table.

In	2	5	8	10	9	6	7	4
Out	20							

Times Tables

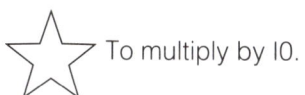 To multiply by 10.

Coins

These are piles of 10p coins. Write down how much money there is in each pile.

 [4] x 10p = [40p]    [ ] x 10p = [ ]

 [ ] x 10p = [ ]    [ ] x 10p = [ ]

 [ ] x 10p = [ ]    [ ] x 10p = [ ]

 [ ] x 10p = [ ]    [ ] x 10p = [ ]

Complete the table.

1 x 10p = 10p	2 x 10p =	3 x 10p =	4 x 10p =	5 x 10p =
6 x 10p =	7 x 10p =	8 x 10p =	9 x 10p =	10 x 10p =

Times Tables

Sixes

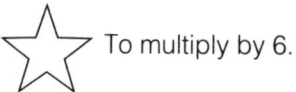 To multiply by 6.

Write in the missing numbers.

 1 hexagon 6 corners 1 x 6 = 6

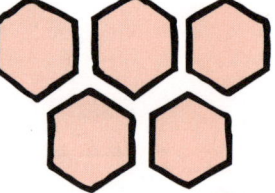 5 hexagons ☐ corners ☐ x 6 = ☐

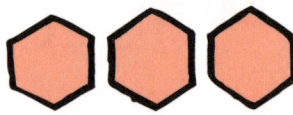 3 hexagons ☐ corners ☐ x 6 = ☐

 6 hexagons ☐ corners ☐ x 6 = ☐

 2 hexagons ☐ corners ☐ x 6 = ☐

Complete the table.

In	4	6	10	8	3	7	9	5
Out	24							

Times Tables

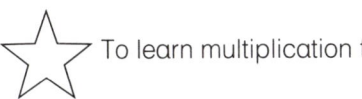 To learn multiplication facts.

Dice

Complete these multiplications.

 x 2 = 10    x 6 = ☐    x 2 = ☐

 x 4 = ☐    x 5 = ☐    x 3 = ☐

Draw the missing spots on these dice.

☐ x 3 = 18   ☐ x 4 = 16   ☐ x 2 = 8

☐ x 3 = 15   ☐ x 5 = 25   ☐ x 6 = 36

Dice Game for two players.

You need two dice, and a set of counters each. Take turns to throw both dice and multiply the numbers together.

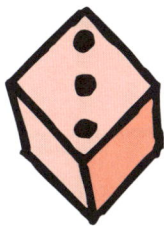

3 x 4 = 12

The player with the larger score takes a counter. The winner is the first to collect 10 counters.

23

Times Tables

Fives, tens, sixes

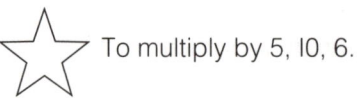 To multiply by 5, 10, 6.

Complete these multiplications.

fives

3 x 5 = 15	5 x 5 =	6 x 5 =
8 x 5 =	10 x 5 =	9 x 5 =
4 x 5 =	7 x 5 =	2 x 5 =

tens

1 x 10 = 10	6 x 10 =	2 x 10 =
4 x 10 =	0 x 10 =	7 x 10 =
8 x 10 =	3 x 10 =	5 x 10 =

sixes

5 x 6 = 30	7 x 6 =	2 x 6 =
9 x 6 =	4 x 6 =	0 x 6 =
1 x 6 =	8 x 6 =	3 x 6 =

Times Tables

 To multiply by 9.

Nines

Write in the missing numbers.

 1 card 9 spots 1 × 9 = 9

 3 cards  ☐ spots ☐ × 9 = ☐

 5 cards 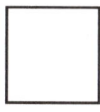 ☐ spots ☐ × 9 = ☐

 4 cards  ☐ spots  ☐ × 9 = ☐

  2 cards  ☐ spots ☐ × 9 = ☐

Complete the table.

In	3	5	10	7	8	9	6	2
Out	27							

25

Times Tables

Eights

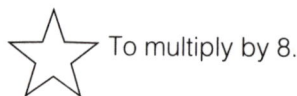 To multiply by 8.

Write in the missing numbers.

 1 octopus [8] legs [1] x 8 = [8]

 6 octopuses [ ] legs [ ] x 8 = [ ]

 3 octopuses [ ] legs [ ] x 8 = [ ]

 2 octopuses [ ] legs [ ] x 8 = [ ]

 4 octopuses [ ] legs [ ] x 8 = [ ]

Complete the table.

In	4	6	9	7	5	10	2	8
Out	32							

Times Tables

 To multiply by 7.

Sevens

Write in the missing numbers.

 1 pod [7] peas [1] x 7 = [7]

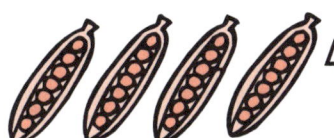 4 pods [   ] peas [   ] x 7 = [   ]

 2 pods [   ] peas [   ] x 7 = [   ]

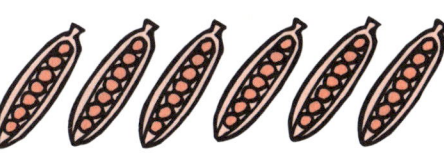 6 pods [   ] peas [   ] x 7 = [   ]

 3 pods [   ] peas [   ] x 7 = [   ]

Complete the table.

In	3	5	7	4	9	8	10	6
Out	21							

Times Tables

Nines, eights, sevens

 To multiply by 9, 8, 7.

Complete these multiplications.

nines

2 x 9 = 18	5 x 9 = ☐	7 x 9 = ☐
6 x 9 = ☐	3 x 9 = ☐	9 x 9 = ☐
8 x 9 = ☐	10 x 9 = ☐	4 x 9 = ☐

eights

3 x 8 = 24	6 x 8 = ☐	5 x 8 = ☐
7 x 8 = ☐	2 x 8 = ☐	10 x 8 = ☐
4 x 8 = ☐	9 x 8 = ☐	8 x 8 = ☐

sevens

1 x 7 = 7	4 x 7 = ☐	6 x 7 = ☐
0 x 7 = ☐	9 x 7 = ☐	3 x 7 = ☐
8 x 7 = ☐	2 x 7 = ☐	7 x 7 = ☐

Times Tables

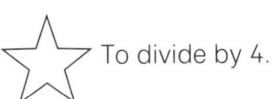 To divide by 4.

Sharing between four

Share these shapes between four by drawing them.

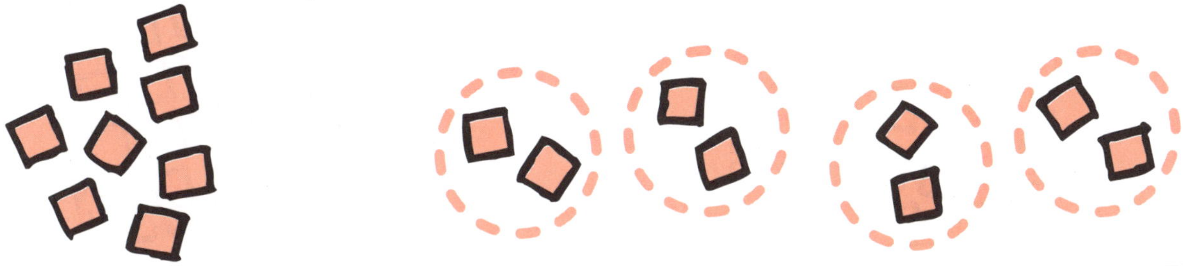

| 8 | shared by 4 is | 2 | each | 8 | ÷ 4 = | 2 |

| 12 | shared by 4 is | 4 | each | | ÷ 4 = | |

| | shared by 4 is | | each | | ÷ 4 = | |

Complete the table. Say each sum when you write it.

4 ÷ 4 = 1	8 ÷ 4 =	12 ÷ 4 =	16 ÷ 4 =	20 ÷ 4 =
24 ÷ 4 =	28 ÷ 4 =	32 ÷ 4 =	36 ÷ 4 =	40 ÷ 4 =

Times Tables

Multiplying

 To learn multiplication facts.

Write these multiplications.

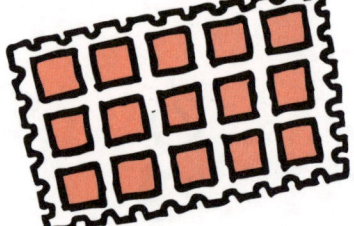

| 3 | x | 5 | = | 15 |

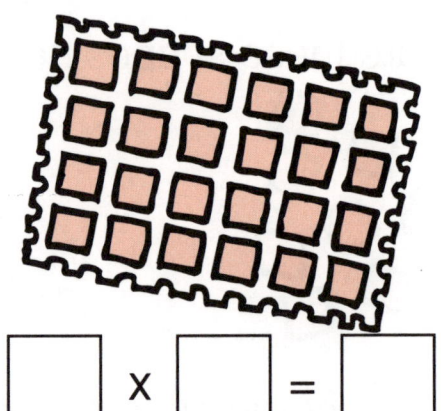

| | x | | = | |

| | x | | = | |

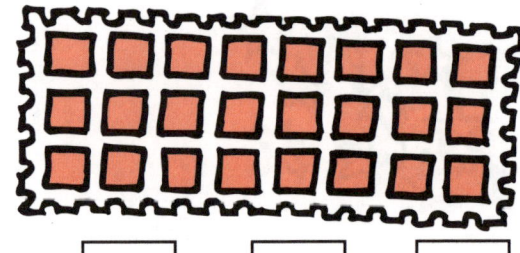

| | x | | = | |

Complete the multiplication tables.

x	3	4	5	6
3	9	12		
4			20	
5				
6		24		

x	2	7	5	9
1		7		
6				
3				27
8		56		

Times Tables

 To learn multiplication facts.

Multiplying

Write these multiplications.

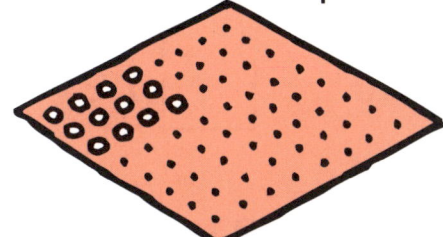

3 × 4 = 12

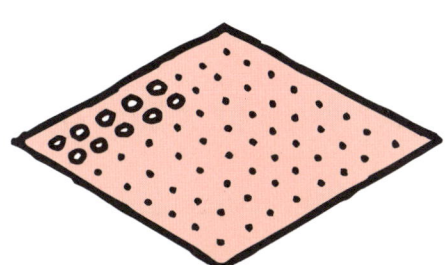

☐ × ☐ = ☐

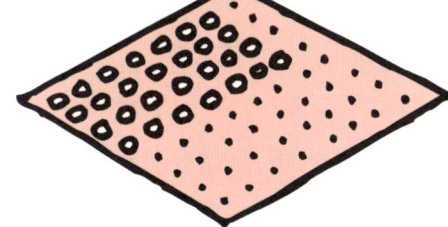

☐ × ☐ = ☐

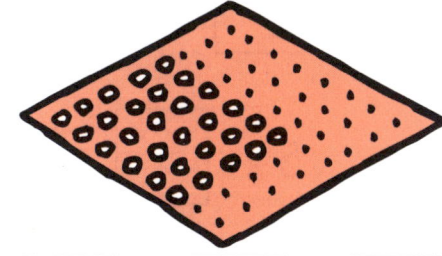

☐ × ☐ = ☐

Complete the multiplication tables.

×	5	6	7	8
5		30		
6				48
7				
8				

×	4	7	8	5
9				
6				
3				
10				

Times Tables

Multiplying

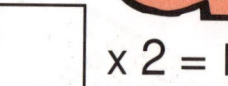 To learn multiplication facts.

Write in the missing numbers.

twos ☐ x 2 = 6   2 x ☐ = 10   ☐ x 2 = 16

threes 3 x ☐ = 15   ☐ x 3 = 12   3 x ☐ = 30

fours ☐ x 4 = 24   4 x ☐ = 32   ☐ x 4 = 12

fives 5 x ☐ = 35   ☐ x 5 = 45   5 x ☐ = 10

sixes ☐ x 6 = 60   6 x ☐ = 30   ☐ x 6 = 6

sevens 7 x ☐ = 0   ☐ x 7 = 63   7 x ☐ = 42

eights ☐ x 8 = 40   8 x ☐ = 32   ☐ x 8 = 64

nines 9 x ☐ = 27   ☐ x 9 = 81   9 x ☐ = 63

tens ☐ x 10 = 60   10 x ☐ = 20   ☐ x 10 = 70